The Church

LIFE IN ELIZABETHAN ENGLAND

The Church

KATHRYN HINDS

MARSHALL CAVENDISH BENCHMARK   NEW YORK

To Jill

The author and publisher specially wish to thank Dr. Megan Lynn Isaac,
former associate professor of Renaissance Literature at Youngstown State University, Ohio,
for her invaluable help in reviewing the manuscript.

MARSHALL CAVENDISH BENCHMARK 99 WHITE PLAINS ROAD TARRYTOWN, NEW YORK 10591-9001
www.marshallcavendish.usText copyright © 2008 by Marshall Cavendish Corporation All rights reserved. No part of this
book may be reproduced or utilized in any form or by any means electronic or mechanical including photocopying,
recording, or by any information storage and retrieval system, without permission from the copyright holders. All Internet
sites were available and accurate when this book was sent to press. LIBRARY OF CONGRESS CATALOGING-IN-PUBLICATION
DATA Hinds, Kathryn, 1962-   The Church / by Kathryn Hinds. p. cm. — (Life in Elizabethan England) Summary: "A
social history of Elizabethan England, focusing on the role religion played in the lives of both the powerful and the ordinary people who lived in England during the famous monarch's reign: 1558-1603"—Provided by publisher. Includes
bibliographical references and index. ISBN 978-0-7614-2545-8 1. Great Britain—Church history—16th century—
Juvenile literature. 2. Great Britain—History—Elizabeth, 1558-1603—Juvenile literature. 3. Great Britain—Religious life
and customs—Juvenile literature. I. Title. II. Series. BR756.H56 2008 274.2'06—dc22 2007009392

EDITOR: Joyce Stanton   PUBLISHER: Michelle Bisson
ART DIRECTOR: Anahid Hamparian   SERIES DESIGNER: Michael Nelson

Images provided by Rose Corbett Gordon, Art Editor, Mystic CT, from the following sources:
Cover: Fine Art Photographic Library/Corbis Back cover: Victoria & Albert Museum, London/Art Resource, NY Pages
1, 12, 33: Private Collection/Stapleton Collection/Bridgeman Art Library; pages 2-3, 36: Rafael Valls Gallery,
London/Bridgeman Art Library; page 6: Sheffield Galleries and Museums Trust/Bridgeman Art Library; page 8: Fine Art
Photographic Library/Corbis; page 10: Bettmann/Corbis; page 11 left & right: Ashmolean Museum, University of
Oxford/Bridgeman Art Library; page 13: Victoria & Albert Museum/Art Resource, NY; pages 14, 72: Fitzwilliam
Museum, University of Cambridge/Bridgeman Art Library; pages 16, 46: Victoria & Albert Museum/Bridgeman Art
Library; pages 18, 35, 38, 49, 63, 68: The Granger Collection, NY; page 20: Yale Center for British Art/Gift of Ann and
Kenneth Rapoport/Bridgeman Art Library; page 21: Michael Maslan Historic Photographs/Corbis; pages 23, 58, 66:
Private Collection/Bridgeman Art Library; page 25: James Morris/Art Resource, NY; page 26: Lebrecht Music & Arts/The
Image Works; page 27: John Minnion/Lebrecht/The Image Works; page 28: Lambeth Palace, London/Bridgeman Art
Library; page 30: Museum of London/Topham-HIP/The Image Works; page 32: Stapleton Collection/Corbis; page 39:
Kingston Lacy, Dorset/National Trust Photographic Library/Derrick E. Witty/Bridgeman Art Library; page 41: Woburn
Abbey, Bedfordshire/Bridgeman Art Library; page 42: Mary Evans Picture Library/The Image Works; pages 43, 44:
Hulton Archive/Getty Images; page 45: Roger_Viollet/The Image Works; page 48: Leeds Museums and Galleries (City Art
Gallery)/ Bridgeman Art Library page 51: Private Collection/Photo Christie's Images/Bridgeman Art Library; page 53: Roy
Miles Fine Paintings/Bridgeman Art Library; page 56: British Library, London/Bridgeman Art Library; page 60: Musee
des Beaux-Arts, Lille, France/Lauros/Giraudon/Bridgeman Art Library; page 65: Beauchamp Collection/Bridgeman Art
Library; page 70: Santa Maria di Castello, Genoa, Italy/Bridgeman Art Library; page 71: Musee Cantonal des Beaux-Arts
de Lausanne, Switzerland/Photo Held Collection/Bridgeman Art Library.

Printed in Malaysia
135642

front cover: Martin Luther, founder of the Protestant Reformation, at work on his translation of the Bible
half-title page: The Bishop of Durham, portrayed in 1825 by Sarah Malden, Countess of Essex
title page: Gathered around their dining table, a family says grace together.
back cover: This miniature may be a portrait of the sixteen-year-old Princess Elizabeth, who would become queen nine years later.

CONTENTS

An elderly woman finds comfort in her Bible.

About Elizabethan England

IT WAS A GOLDEN AGE: A TIME OF POETRY, THEATER, AND SONG; intrigue, adventure, and exploration; faith, intellect, and passion; trials, triumphs, and splendor. The reign of Elizabeth I, from 1558 to 1603, was like no other era of English history. Under Elizabeth's leadership, England began the journey from small, isolated, poor island nation to thriving world power. Under the poets and playwrights of Elizabeth's time—above all, William Shakespeare—the English language reached new heights, and a powerful body of literature was created, one that still delights and inspires us. Elizabeth invited and influenced other forms of creativity as well, and her rule left indelible marks not only in the arts but in politics, religion, and society. The glories—and the troubles—of her reign are all part of the heritage shared by England and its former colonies.

This series of books looks at the Elizabethan age with a focus on its people and their everyday lives, whether they were at the top of society, the bottom, or somewhere in the middle. We will see how they worked, where they lived, how they related to one another, how they relaxed and celebrated special occasions, how they coped with life's hardships. In this volume we will learn about the roles that religion played in the lives of Elizabethans, from the queen and her court to bishops and priests to ordinary women and men. These people had many of the same joys and sorrows, hopes and fears that we do. They were poised at the beginning of the modern age, but still their world was very different from ours. Forget about telephones, computers, cars, and televisions, and step back in time. . . . Welcome to life in Elizabethan England!

The Church of England

O Lord our heavenly father, . . . most heartily we beseech thee with thy favor
to behold our most gracious sovereign lady Queen Elizabeth. . . . Grant her in
health and wealth long to live; strengthen her that she may vanquish and
overcome all her enemies. And finally after this life she may
attain everlasting joy and felicity.
—THE BOOK OF COMMON PRAYER, 1559

THE SIXTEENTH CENTURY WAS A TUMULTUOUS TIME in Europe. The recently invented printing press was changing the way people communicated and passed on knowledge. Printed books and pamphlets made a wide range of ideas available to people in larger numbers than ever before. Among these ideas, two were of momentous importance: humanism and reform. Humanism sought to revive the learning and philosophy of the ancient Greeks and Romans and, ultimately, to surpass their achievements in the arts and sciences. Reform applied to the church, which some people believed had become corrupt. In 1517 the German monk Martin Luther started a protest against many church practices, and this led to the split of the western European church into Catholic and Protestant ("protesting") branches. A century and more of religious struggle followed.

Opposite: The parish church was an important center of community life in the towns and villages of Elizabethan England.

9

Martin Luther started a religious movement that would profoundly influence European history, culture, and society.

When Luther began the Reformation, or reform movement, England's ruler was Henry VIII. At first Henry defended the Catholic Church. Later, for personal and political reasons, he broke away from it to found the Church of England, or Anglican Church, a Protestant denomination with himself at its head. As king after him, his young son Edward strengthened English Protestantism. Edward ruled only six years and was succeeded by his half sister Mary, a devout Catholic. She declared England a Catholic country once more and persecuted many Protestants who refused to change their faith. Mary reigned for five years. When she died, the last of Henry's children came to the throne: Elizabeth.

ELIZABETH'S RELIGIOUS SETTLEMENT

Elizabeth knew that one of the first things she had to do for her country was settle the question of its religion once and for all. In sixteenth-century Europe, it was a widely accepted idea that religious unity and national unity went hand in hand. As Elizabeth's leading councillor, William Cecil, expressed it, "That state could never be in safety where there was toleration of two religions." All the people should belong to the same church, which would both support the government and be supported by it. And it was the ruler's right and responsibility to decide which church the nation belonged to.

The people of England were divided in their religious loyalties. There were large numbers of both Catholics and Anglicans, as well as a significant minority of Puritans. These were Protestants who wanted to "purify" church and society, reforming both strictly according to the Bible. Elizabeth herself was a Protestant who continued to prefer many features of Catholic worship. Moreover, she was an extremely well-educated humanist, who read Greek and Latin as easily as English and was very familiar with ancient history and philosophy. These factors, combined with her personality and political sense, compelled her to take a practical approach in finding the religious solution that she felt would most benefit her country.

One thing that almost everyone in England could agree on was that they did not want any foreign power interfering in their affairs. To Protestants and even to many Catholics, the pope, head of the Catholic Church, was such a power: he lived in Rome, he ruled much of Italy like a prince, and nearly all the popes during this period were Italians. Italy's interests were not England's, so why should an Italian prince have any influence in England? Because of feelings like this, most of Elizabeth's people liked, or at least accepted, the idea of an English church run by English churchmen under the authority of the English monarch.

A couple dressed in the sober style favored by Puritans in the early 1600s

Other decisions were harder. Before the Reformation, Catholic practices had been followed throughout western Europe for more than a thousand years. Even people who did not necessarily believe many teachings of the Catholic Church found it difficult to give up the old ways of doing things. On the other hand, the Puritans wanted to sweep away everything that even hinted of Catholicism.

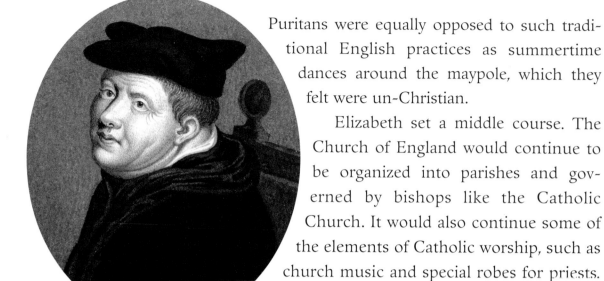

Edmund Bonner, Bishop of London, was responsible for much of the persecution of Protestants during Mary's reign. When Elizabeth became queen, he refused to take the Oath of Supremacy and so spent the rest of his life in prison.

Puritans were equally opposed to such traditional English practices as summertime dances around the maypole, which they felt were un-Christian.

Elizabeth set a middle course. The Church of England would continue to be organized into parishes and governed by bishops like the Catholic Church. It would also continue some of the elements of Catholic worship, such as church music and special robes for priests. But while Catholic services were in Latin, the Church of England would conduct its services in English. Anglican priests, unlike Catholic ones, would be allowed to marry (although Elizabeth preferred them not to, especially in the higher ranks). There would be no monasteries, no monks or nuns, as there were in Catholicism. Fewer saints (holy people) and saints' days would be recognized and celebrated. And, in place of the pope, the English monarch would have ultimate authority over the English church.

SUPREMACY AND UNIFORMITY

Elizabeth reestablished the Church of England with the help of Parliament, which passed the Acts of Supremacy and Uniformity in April 1559. The first was "an act restoring to the crown the ancient jurisdiction over the state ecclesiastical [the church] and spiritual and abolishing all foreign power repugnant [opposed] to the same." This act required all church and government officials to place a hand on the Bible and swear the Oath of Supremacy:

> I . . . do utterly testify and declare in my conscience that the queen's highness is the only supreme governor of this realm . . . as well in all spiritual and ecclesiastical things or causes as temporal [worldly], and that no foreign prince, person, prelate [clergyman], state, or potentate [ruler] hath or ought to have any jurisdiction, power, superiority, pre-eminence, or authority, ecclesiastical or spiritual, within this realm.

The Act of Supremacy also made it illegal for anyone in Elizabeth's realm (which included Wales as well as England) to write, print, teach, preach, or otherwise express support for any kind of foreign authority over the English church.

Queen Elizabeth in 1572, portrayed by Nicholas Hilliard, one of her favorite artists

The Act of Uniformity required that all English church services follow a slightly revised version of the Book of Common Prayer that had been authorized by Parliament and Elizabeth's half brother, Edward VI, in 1552. The act also set penalties for clergymen who used any other form of worship, for anyone who compelled or convinced a clergymen to use another form of worship, and for anyone who "shall in any Enterludes, Plays, Songs, Rhymes, or by other open Words, declare or speak anything in the derogation, depraving, or despising of the same Book or of anything therein contained." In addition, the Act of Uniformity decreed that every person in England must go to church every Sunday and holy day. Missing a service without a good excuse

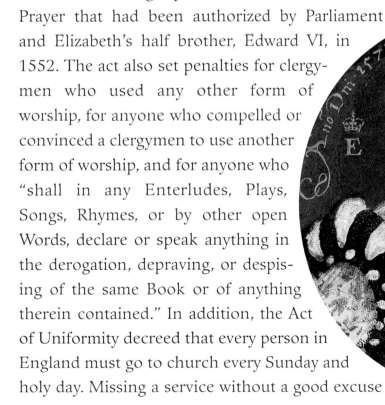

CHRISTIAN BASICS

Catholic or Protestant, English Christians shared basic beliefs. Most important, the center of their faith was Jesus. According to the New Testament of the Bible, Jesus was sent by God to save humanity from its sins. The Bible described Jesus's birth and one episode from his childhood, and then picked up his story at about the age of thirty. At this time, Jesus went to his cousin John for baptism, a ceremony in which John symbolically cleansed people of their past sins so that they could begin to live more righteous lives. Jesus spent the next three years performing miracles, healing the sick, and teaching. He attracted a large number of followers, both women and men. Twelve of these followers, called the disciples or apostles, were his most devoted students. Then Jesus was arrested for rebellion. Condemned to death by the Romans, he was crucified, or executed by being hung on a cross. Three days later, some of his women followers went to his tomb and found it empty. An angel told them that Jesus had been resurrected—he had risen from the dead. All English Christians believed in the authority of the New Testament and its promises that Jesus had died for humanity's sins and that through him people could have eternal life with God. These basics were what mattered to Elizabeth, who once told a French ambassador, "There is only one Jesus Christ. The rest is a dispute over trifles."

Above: Jesus carrying the cross to his place of execution.
On the lower left his mother, Mary, is comforted by Saint John, one of the twelve disciples.

(such as illness) would result in a fine of twelve pence, roughly one week's pay for the average worker.

THE ANGLICAN WAY

The Book of Common Prayer was a means of uniting the English people in a shared system of approved belief and worship. As its preface explained,

> Of necessity there must be some rules, therefore certain rules are here set forth. . . . Here are left out many things, whereof some be untrue, some uncertain, some vain and superstitious, and is ordained nothing to be read but . . . the holy scriptures, or that which is evidently grounded upon the same. . . . Where heretofore there hath been great diversity in saying and singing in churches within this realm, . . . now from henceforth, all the whole realm shall have but one use.

The Book of Common Prayer was designed to be the only book needed in English churches besides the Bible. It laid out all the regular services to be held: morning and evening prayer every day, with extra prayers on Wednesdays and Fridays and an extended morning service on Sundays. The prayer book also contained a schedule of Bible readings so that, with all the services combined, in every church the whole book of Psalms would be read each month, the New Testament four times a year, and the Old Testament once a year. In addition, the Book of Common Prayer contained services for particular occasions, such as baptisms, weddings, and funerals. There were also prayers to help people through times of war, sickness, famine, and other hardships.

To make sure that all churches switched over to the Book of

THE ARTICLES OF FAITH

To solidify the Church of England's position, in 1566 Parliament passed an act requiring all English clergy to abide by the Thirty-nine Articles. Also known as the Articles of Faith, these were (and still are) statements of the official teachings of the Anglican Church.* They include belief in:

• The Holy Trinity, the three united Persons of the Godhead: God the Father, God the Son (Jesus), and God the Holy Ghost (or Holy Spirit).
• Jesus as divine and human at the same time, and his sacrifice for people's sins.
• The authority of both the Old and New Testaments of the Bible, which contain everything people need to know for salvation.
• Original sin—humans are naturally sinful; Jesus alone was without sin, and humans can only do good through the grace of God.
• Justification by faith—humans are redeemed from sin only by faith in Jesus; good works spring from faith but cannot earn salvation.

*The full Thirty-nine Articles can be found in all current editions of the Book of Common Prayer. They can also be read online at http://www.fordham.edu/halsall/mod/1571-39articles.html

Above: A stained-glass window in an English church depicts the story of Jesus's birth in a manger.

Common Prayer, Elizabeth and her Privy Council issued the Injunctions of 1559, which outlined the specifics of how the Church of England would be run. A group of royal commissioners traveled throughout England and Wales with copies of the Injunctions, visiting religious leaders in every region. It was a peaceful transition, and nearly all the clergy agreed to the Acts of Supremacy and Uniformity and to follow the Injunctions.

With the process of reestablishing the Church of England well under way, the Duke of Norfolk cautioned Elizabeth, "Let your Highness assure yourself that England can bear no more changes in religion, it hath been bowed so oft that if it should be bent again it would break." She knew this well. Her religious settlement was designed to assure peace, stability, and unity in her realm, and she worked tirelessly to preserve this state of harmony. She was mainly successful, especially if England was compared to many other nations of Europe, where religious warfare was becoming increasingly common. In 1580 an official named Sir Walter Mildmay described the situation vividly: In France, Germany, and elsewhere, there were "depopulations and devastations of whole provinces and countries, overthrowing, spoiling and sacking of cities and towns, imprisoning, ransoming and murdering of all kind of people"—but in England, "the peaceable government of her Majesty doth make us to enjoy all that is ours in more freedom than any nation under the sun at this day."

2

Church and Community

*Almighty God will have his house and place whither the whole parish and
congregation shall resort, which is called the church and temple of God,
for that the church, which is the company of God's people,
doth there assemble and come together to serve him.*

— "HOMILY ON REPAIRING AND KEEPING CLEAN THE CHURCH," 1562

ONE THING THAT MADE THE REESTABLISHMENT OF THE Church of England proceed so smoothly was that Elizabeth and her councillors did not try to change the existing religious structure. The Catholic Church was extremely well organized, with every part of Christian Europe divided up into administrative units by region. The basic division was the parish. A group of neighboring parishes made up a diocese, overseen by a bishop, and a group of dioceses formed an archdiocese, governed by an archbishop. The Anglican Church kept this system of leadership by bishops, which is why its offshoots in other countries are often called Episcopalian—the Latin for "bishop" is *episcopus*.

Opposite: Saint Paul's was one of the most important churches in Elizabethan London. Its tall spire rises high above the city in this woodcut from the early 1500s.

19

The Importance of Order

The structure of the church and its government by bishops made sense and seemed proper to most Elizabethans. This was what they were used to and, moreover, it was in harmony with the value they placed on rank and order. One of the period's most famous expressions of the importance of order, or "degree," comes from Shakespeare's play *Troilus and Cressida*:

> The heavens themselves, the planets, and this centre
> Observe degree, priority, and place,
> Infixture, course, proportion, season, form,
> Office and custom, in all line of order. . . .
> . . . O when degree is shaked,
> Which is the ladder to all high designs,
> The enterprise is sick. How could communities,
> Degrees in schools, and brotherhoods in cities,
> Peaceful commerce from dividable shores,
> The primogenity* and due of birth,
> Prerogative** of age, crowns, sceptres, laurels,
> But by degree stand in authentic place?
> Take but degree away, untune that string,
> And hark what discord follows. . . .

*the right of the firstborn son to inherit

**privilege, power

Even when praying at a funeral, Elizabethans observed rules of conduct based on rank and order.

Lord Leycester Hospital in the town of Warwick was founded by Queen Elizabeth's friend the Earl of Leicester in 1571 as an act of charity. The hospital provided housing and care for elderly or disabled soldiers and their wives.

THE PARISH

Parish basically means "neighborhood"; this was the local community. Each parish had its own church building and cemetery. Usually a country village would be a single parish, serving all the people within walking or riding distance. Sometimes, though, a parish was made up of several villages. Then there might be one or more chapels in different parts of the parish, so that people could go to them if the main church was too far or too difficult to get to. A city would have many parishes—London had more than a hundred. An average-size London parish was probably fifty or so households. In all, there were about 13,000 parishes in Elizabethan England.

As a neighborhood, the parish was a social unit as well as a religious one. It also played an important role in aspects of government. For example, each parish had to provide and equip a certain number of men to serve in the local militia. These citizen-soldiers were called up periodically to march and train together for two or three days. They could also be summoned to serve an indefinite time in the armies that Elizabeth sent to Ireland and the Low Countries, but their most important role was to be ready to defend England in case of invasion.

The parish was also responsible for taking care of its poor. It had to find work for those who were able-bodied and provide support for those who weren't. The work was often spinning: the parish would regularly give people an amount of flax or wool to spin and then buy the resulting thread, paying according to the quality of the workmanship. Some of the needy were given much more unpleasant jobs. For instance, during times of plague, a parish might pay an old widow to take food to those who were quarantined with the infection and to report deaths when they occurred.

Chief among the poor who could not support themselves were children, especially orphans. Some places had "foundling hospitals," or orphanages, where these children could be taken care of and taught useful skills. Otherwise the parish generally found a respectable family to foster one or more children and provided some money every year to help pay for their food and clothing. This assistance was mainly financed by donations from well-to-do parishioners (who were required by law to give a certain minimum amount) and the fines collected from people who didn't attend church on Sunday. The parish could also use its "poor fund" to give people emergency assistance and provide other one-time needs. Parish account books have left records of such needs and their expenses, in many cases hinting at stories of great hardship and sadness, as in the case of this entry from a London parish: "[for] a sheet and for bearers to carry a poor Irish woman to church, which died in Fawkes Hall, 20d*; for victuals [food] for her children, 14d; for the grave making and for the clerk, 6d; for burying one of her children, 6d."

*d is the abbreviation for *pence*.

The Church

Saint Paul's is a focal point in a royal procession winding its way through London.

HOUSES OF WORSHIP

Just as parishes served multiple purposes, church buildings could be used for meetings, schools, law courts, and musters of the militia. Churchyards were often the sites of dances, games (lawn bowling, for example), and other outdoor gatherings, while market stalls were frequently set up in the area around a cathedral. Many people, especially Puritans, disapproved of churchyard dances and such, but otherwise accepted the various uses of the church, since it was often the only local place where a large number of people could gather. And since it was meant to be the center of the community, what was more natural than it functioning as a kind of community center? Nevertheless, the church building was primarily a house of worship. A sermon summed up the ideal this way:

Churches were made . . . to serve God truly, there to learn his blessed will, there to call upon his mighty name, there to use the holy sacraments, there to travail [work at] how to be in charity [Christian love] with thy neighbor, there to have thy poor and needy neighbor in remembrance, from thence to depart better and more godly than thou camest thither.

England and Wales were full of churches, often many hundreds of years old, and the Elizabethans did not feel the need to build new ones. The existing buildings, however, did have to undergo some changes to make them fit for the Church of England. Altars were to be replaced by communion tables. All paintings, carvings, and statues of saints and of Jesus on the cross had to be removed, along with many other kinds of decorations. These things were felt to be too great a temptation to the sin of idolatry, the worshipping of images. A sermon contrasted the use of statues and other Catholic customs with the goals of the Anglican Church:

Let us honor and worship for religion's sake none but him [God], and let us worship and honor as he . . . hath declared by his word, that he will be honored and worshipped, not in nor by images or idols, which he hath most straightly forbidden, neither in kneeling, lighting of candles, burning of incense, offering up of gifts unto images and idols, . . . but let us honor and worship God in spirit and truth, fearing and

loving him above all things, trusting in him only, calling upon him, and praying to him only.

The sermon writer knew that many people said images in churches were "the laymen's books"—that is, that people who did not have the education of the clergy could still learn about the faith by "reading" the pictures and statues. But, he argued, since "no true image of God, our saviour Christ, or his saints can be made," images teach "lies and errors. Wherefore either they be no books, or if they be, they be false and lying books, the teachers of all error."

The Church of England preferred real books—specifically the books of the Bible. Instead of paintings, church walls were now decorated with Bible verses, and from 1561 on, according to law, all churches had to display the Ten Commandments. The

A choir of men and boys share a large music book as they sing one of the Psalms in church.

increased emphasis on the word of God required other changes, too. Author and clergyman William Harrison summed up some of them in his 1587 *Description of England*:

Whereas there was wont [accustomed] to be a great partition between the choir and the body of the church, now it is either very small or none at all, and, to say the truth, altogether needless, sith [since] the minister saith his service commonly in the body of the church, with his face toward the people . . . ; by which means the ignorant do not only

The Church

learn divers [a number] of the psalms and usual prayers by heart, but also such as can read do pray together with him.

Church music was also affected. It was much simplified, to make sure that all the words the choir sang could easily be understood by the congregation. Many parishes, especially where there was strong Puritan influence, also did away with organ music. Queen Elizabeth, however, loved elaborate and beautiful church music. Two of the organists she employed in the royal chapel were among the greatest composers England has produced, Thomas Tallis and William Byrd. Tallis's hymns and other music are still frequently used in Anglican and Episcopal churches today. And Elizabeth's chapel choir was so superb that a French ambassador wrote, "In all my travels in France, Italy, and Spain, I never heard the like: a concert of music so excellent and sweet as cannot be expressed."

Composer and organist William Byrd was a Catholic, but Elizabeth protected him and employed him in her chapel because she found his music so beautiful and inspiring.

3

𝔐en of 𝔊od

They ought to excel all other in purity of life, and should be examples to the people
to live well and Christianly.
⟶ THE INJUNCTIONS OF 1559

THE CHURCH OF ENGLAND HAD A HIERARCHY, OR structure by rank, of clergy. The highest-level churchman was the archbishop of Canterbury, followed by the archbishop of York. Beneath them were the bishops, who governed the twenty-seven dioceses of England and Wales. Each bishop had his headquarters in a cathedral, a large and splendid church that took its name from the fact that it housed the bishop's throne, or *cathedra* in Latin. A bishop was responsible for supervising all the priests or ministers in his diocese.

LORDS OF THE CHURCH

Bishops and archbishops were equal in rank to nobles. In fact, they were called "lords spiritual," and they held seats in Parliament's House of Lords. They often lived like lords, too. Their official resi-

Opposite: Matthew Parker, Elizabeth's first archbishop of Canterbury, shared her love of scholarship and her dislike of religious extremism. He helped put her religious settlement into action and gave it a solid foundation.

dences were palaces, and they usually had manors and other property in various places, both in their dioceses and elsewhere in England or Wales. Most, however, were not of noble birth. A number were the sons of gentlemen, but the majority were from the middle class—the sons of merchants, craftsmen, and well-to-do farmers.

The archbishop of Canterbury's London residence, where he could be close to the center of government, was Lambeth Palace. His household was large. Archbishop Matthew Parker, for example, who served from 1559 to 1575, kept more than sixty servants and retainers. Among these were secretaries, a treasurer, a doctor, a man in charge of giving out donations to the poor, a cook, chaplains, stable keepers, personal attendants, and a steward to oversee them all. The archbishop and his family lived in the palace's private apartments, but he dined publicly in the great hall three times a week, playing host to local and visiting dignitaries. Parker, who had been a professor at Cambridge University, especially enjoyed welcoming scholars to Lambeth. With the help of his learned friends and colleagues, Parker collected, edited, and published

The Church

many medieval manuscripts. He also made a hobby of genealogy.

Bishops had many duties focused on the day-to-day running of their dioceses, each of which they or their representatives visited every few years. They were responsible for licensing schoolmasters, doctors, and midwives. Bishops also were in charge of the church courts, which exercised authority over wills and marriages, disciplined priests, enforced moral behavior, and tried people accused of breaking religious rules. The bishops' courts dealt with matters large and small. For example, one priest was fined for allowing a puppet show to be performed in his church; another was disciplined for not having a Bible in his. A man who accused a fellow parishioner of a crime without enough evidence was ordered to make a public confession of his sins. A woman who missed church because it was the only time she could do her laundry was told that wouldn't excuse her from paying the fine. Another woman was brought into the bishop's court for singing naughty rhymes about her neighbors.

The Parish Priest

A common clergyman in the Church of England might be called a priest, minister, pastor, parson, rector, vicar, or curate. Some terms were used interchangeably, while others referred to how the man was appointed to his parish and how he was paid for his work. For example, a rector or vicar was selected by a patron, which could be a bishop, a nobleman, an organization (such as a college), or the queen herself. Such an appointment was called a benefice or living, and it entitled the holder to receive tithes, taxes paid to the church by all English citizens.

Tithes were sometimes paid in money, but in the countryside they usually took the form of grain, hay, livestock, poultry, fish—whatever the products of the parish were. Tithes were classified as

This sixteenth-century woodcut depicts townsmen coming to an official's home to pay their taxes.

"greater" or "lesser," depending on how important the various products were to the local economy. Rectors received the greater, and vicars the lesser. Curates, however, were appointed by rectors or vicars and did not share in the tithes. Instead a curate received a small annual salary, which he often had to supplement in order to support himself and his family.

The parish supplied its minister with a house called a parsonage (or rectory or vicarage). In rural areas, the parsonage had gardens and orchards, so the minister and his family could grow some of their own food. The parish church also owned a plot of farmland called the glebe. The minister could choose to rent this out or farm it himself. One hardworking rector, well pleased with his parsonage gardens and his decision to work his glebe, wrote, "By this means I have sustained a greater family, I have entertained my richer neighbours more bountifully, and have not been unmindful to relieve the poor." It did not do, however, to become *too* enthusiastic about farming and raising livestock, as a bishop's court reported of a certain vicar in 1572: "He is a common cow-keep and one that useth commonly to drive beasts through the town . . . and in other open places, in a jerkin* with a bill** on his neck, not like a prelate [priest] but rather like a common rogue."

Clergymen had the same flaws, both minor and serious, as other people. But since they were held up to higher standards, their fail-

*a hip-length vest or jacket, often made of leather
**a tool with a hooked end, like a bird's bill, for digging, pruning, or cutting

PARISH OFFICERS

Priests did not run their parishes on their own; they needed other men to help. So every parish had its officers. The greatest responsibility belonged to the parish clerk, who was the only officer paid for his work. He kept the parish records, including the register of all baptisms, weddings, and funerals. Next to him in importance were the churchwardens. There were two of them, elected every year during Easter time by the men of the congregation. Churchwardens were generally well-to-do farmers, among the parish's leading citizens. They looked after the parish's finances and made sure the church building was kept in good repair. They were also responsible for the care of the parish poor (with assistance, after 1601, from officials called Poor Law overseers) and were supposed to see to the upkeep of the parish roads and similar matters. The churchwardens had unpaid assistants and hired church employees such as bell ringers and a sexton (responsible for digging graves and similar matters). Justices of the peace, too, played a role in the life of the parish. As part of their duties to promote local law and order, they helped enforce church rules and make decisions about care for orphans and the poor. Like other officials, they were required to swear the Oath of Supremacy. As Elizabeth's reign went on, the oath also became mandatory for all teachers, university graduates, and lawyers.

Above: Bell ringers work together with precise timing to produce a melodious peal of church bells.

ings often came in for extra criticism. In Shakespeare's *Hamlet*, one of the characters points out the hypocrisy of some ministers:

> Do not, as some ungracious pastors do,
> Show me the steep and thorny way to heaven
> Whilst like a puffed and reckless libertine
> Himself the primrose path of dalliance treads
> And recks not his own rede.　　　[and ignores his own advice]

The Injunctions of 1559 dealt with ministers who neglected their duties for inappropriate pastimes:

> Ecclesiastical persons shall in no wise at any unlawful time, nor for any other cause, than for their honest necessities, haunt or resort to any taverns or alehouses. . . . They shall not give themselves to drinking or riot, spending their time idly by day and by night at dice, cards, or tables [backgammon] playing, . . . but at all times, as they shall have leisure, they shall hear or read somewhat of Holy Scripture, or shall occupy themselves with some other honest study.

Most priests, it seems, did perform their duties conscientiously, often becoming a great help and inspiration to their communities. One such was Dr. John Favour, vicar of a poor parish in northern England. In his memoir he wrote of "preaching every Sabbath day, lecturing every day in the week, exercising justice in the commonwealth, practising physic [medicine] and chirurgery [surgery] in the great penury [poverty] and necessity thereof in the country where I live." Like many a rural minister, Dr. Favour cared not just for his flock's spiritual needs: he acted as a lawyer and doctor, he worked to found and fund a grammar school, he saw that clothes and sheets were distributed to the poor, he helped many of his parishioners get work making cloth, and more.

John Favour also encouraged the priests of neighboring parishes to develop their skills at giving sermons by holding a monthly gathering at which they all preached. Such "exercises" or "prophesyings," as they were called, were promoted by Puritan-leaning ministers and bishops, but the queen did not like them. She and many government and church leaders feared that once a preacher got going, he might say whatever came into his head, whether it agreed with approved teachings or not. For this reason, any minister who wanted to preach had to get a license from his bishop, after proving that he was sufficiently knowledgeable in the Bible and the Anglican Church's accepted beliefs.

Many ministers, especially in the first decades of the Elizabethan settlement, were not well-enough educated to do this. The Injunctions of 1559 took the situation into account: "Because through lack of preachers in many places of the queen's realms and dominions the people continue in ignorance and blindness, all parsons, vicars, and curates shall read in their churches every Sunday one of the Homilies [sermons], which are and shall be set forth for the same purpose by the queen's authority." The sermons in the official Book of Homilies (joined by a second volume in 1562) employed Bible verses, the history of early Christianity, and reasoned persuasion to explain the basic beliefs of the Church of England. The Injunctions instructed ministers to read out these sermons "leisurely, plainly, and distinctly"—and if they weren't very good readers, they should practice reading aloud beforehand.

George Herbert is famous as a poet of the early 1600s, but he was also a priest in the Church of England. In his country parish he preached, wrote poetry celebrating God's love, used his own funds to renovate the church, and cared so well for his parishioners that they called him "Holy Mr. Herbert."

Ætatis suæ 39.
1598.

Women and the Church

*From woman sprang man's salvation. A woman
was the first that believed.*
— JANE ANGER, 1589

CATHOLICISM HAD GIVEN WOMEN—AT LEAST SOME women—the possibility of becoming a nun. In Protestantism, though, there was no similar opportunity for a religious career. Women were not allowed to preach, to lead prayers, or to take any other official role in the Anglican Church. The only exception to this was the queen. As Supreme Governor of the church, she could overrule even the archbishop of Canterbury. In fact, when the second man to hold this position during her reign, Edmund Grindal, defied her by supporting "prophesyings," she confined him to Lambeth Palace and directed the bishops herself for the next five years.

THE PROTESTANT IDEAL
Nearly all women in Elizabethan England expected to marry and have children, and most did. The church taught that this was a religious

Opposite: Most Elizabethans believed that women's chief religious role was to bear children and raise them to be good Christians.

duty so that, in the words of "An Homilie of the state of Matrimonie,"

the church of God and his kingdom might . . . be conserved and enlarged, not only in that God giveth children by his blessing, but also in that they be brought up by the parents godly . . . that thus the knowledge of God and true religion might be delivered by succession from one to another that finally many might enjoy that everlasting immortality.

Eve offers the forbidden fruit to Adam in this scene from a fifteenth-century stained-glass window in York Minster cathedral.

The homily went on to discuss the biblical guidelines that married women should follow: "Thus doth Saint Peter preach to them, 'Ye wives, be ye in subjection to obey your own husbands' (1 Peter 3.1). . . . Saint Paul expresseth it in this form of words, 'Let women be subject to their husbands as to the Lord: for the husband is the head of the woman, as Christ is the head of the Church' (Ephesians 5.22–23)."

Churchmen also cited the biblical story of Adam and Eve as a reason for women's position. In the Old Testament book of Genesis, Eve was tempted by a snake to defy God and eat the forbidden fruit of the Tree of Knowledge. As punishment for her disobedience, God decreed that she would suffer pain in childbirth and be ruled by her husband—and so would all women after her.

Law, custom, and religion all agreed in placing wives under the control of their husbands. For their part, husbands were exhorted to care tenderly for their wives, since women were considered the "weaker vessel" and their minds were not believed to be as strong as men's. Therefore a man ought to be gentle, kind, and reasonable with his wife, helping her to understand the Bible, the church's teachings, and the best way to carry out her household duties. All writers seem to have agreed that no man should ever beat his wife: "He thereby setteth forward the devil's work" and "that is the greatest shame that can be," says the homily on matrimony. But many wives were beaten nonetheless, and women were not allowed to divorce abusive husbands. Often they were simply told, "if thou canst suffer an extreme husband, thou shalt have a great reward" in heaven.

A religious woman's life centered on obedience to her husband, care for their children, prayer, and study of the scriptures. The Injunctions of 1559 told ministers to exhort their parishioners—men, women, and children alike—to read the Bible. Before this, few girls and women were encouraged to read, so this change must have been very liberating. Many women found great comfort and enjoyment in their religious studies, and in sharing them with their husbands. Author Philip Stubbs wrote of his wife, Katherine,

> You could seldom or never have come into her
> house and have found her without a Bible or
> some other good book in her hands. And when
> she was not reading, she would spend the time
> in conferring, talking, and reasoning with her
> husband, of the word of God and of religion,
> asking him, what is the sense of this place [in
> scripture], and what is the sense of that? . . .
> She obeyed the commandment of the Apostle
> [Saint Paul], who biddeth women to be silent,
> and to learn of their husbands at home.

Elizabeth Cooke was well educated and influential, as were all her sisters. They married high-ranking men and made English translations of important Protestant works written in French, Italian, and Latin.

Except for participating in group prayers and hymns, women were indeed expected to be silent in church, and they were discouraged from voicing their opinions elsewhere. Some women, however, were able to express their religious feelings in writing. The queen herself set an example for this by having a book of prayers she had written published in 1563. In 1582 a male editor printed *Monument of Matrons,* a collection of prayers and devotional poems by women. Several women successfully published their translations of religious works by French, Swiss, and German Protestants. Lady Mary Sidney Herbert worked with her brother Sir Philip Sidney on a poetic translation of the Psalms; it was not published, but handwritten copies were passed around among the Sidneys' friends and acquaintances. Most women's writing, though, was private, limited to letters and diaries. In the early 1600s Lady Anne Southwell wrote this witty poem in her journal:

> All married men desire to have good wives:
> but few give good example by their lives.
> They are our head; they would have us their heels.
> This makes the good wife kick; the good man reels.
> When God brought Eve to Adam for a bride,
> The text says she was ta'en from out man's side.
> A symbol of that side whose sacred blood*
> Flowed for his Spouse, the Church's, saving good.
> This is a mystery, perhaps too deep
> For blockish Adam that was fallen asleep.

WOMEN UNDER SUSPICION

A woman who spoke her mind too boldly or got "uppity" could find

*This refers to the biblical story of a Roman soldier wounding Jesus in the side as he hung on the cross. The following line refers to the concept of the church being the bride of Christ.

The Church

BIBLICAL WOMEN

In Catholic Europe, the most important of all the saints was Mary, the mother of Jesus. Protestants downplayed Mary's role, but she was still held in great honor, as were several other biblical women. In the New Testament, there was Elizabeth, the mother of John the Baptist, and Mary Magdalene, the first person to see Jesus after he rose from the dead and to believe in the Resurrection. Old Testament women particularly esteemed by Elizabethans included Sarah, the wife of Abraham (the founding father of the Jewish people and, later, the spiritual father of Christians and Muslims); Deborah, a judge and prophet who led the ancient Israelites; Judith, who saved an Israelite city by beheading an invading general; and Esther, a Jewish queen whose cleverness kept her people from being massacred. These last three particularly inspired Queen Elizabeth, giving her and her people role models for strong female leadership. Elizabeth drew on that inspiration in this prayer she wrote early in her reign:

Thou hast done me so special and so rare a mercy that, being a woman by my nature weak, timid, and delicate, as are all women, Thou hast caused me to be vigorous, brave, and strong . . . persist, in giving me strength so that I, like another Deborah, like another Judith, like another Esther, may free Thy people.

Above: The famous Armada Portrait of victorious Queen Elizabeth, made after her navy stopped a Spanish invasion in 1588

The cruel "scold's bridle" was used to punish outspoken women into the 1700s both in England and its American colonies.

herself in trouble, especially if she was poor and had no influential family or friends. At the least, she might be scorned and ridiculed by her neighbors. If she was quarrelsome, very gossipy, or used abusive language, she could face a harsher punishment, from being put in the stocks to having to wear a torturous iron contraption called a "scold's bridle." The device was a muzzle or cage for the head, and it had an iron bit projecting into the mouth and resting on the tongue. The bit was often studded with spikes, so if the "nag" dared to speak she would feel severe pain. If she didn't venture to talk, the bit would inflict just a minimum of pain. The scold, or nagging woman, would have to wear this bridle in public for a time, as punishment for her free speech. In some circumstances, such an outspoken woman might even be accused of being a witch.

The religious turmoil of the 1500s set off waves of fear and mistrust throughout western Europe. Women's roles were changing, too, as more learned to read and write. And during this period there were several prominent and controversial royal women, among them France's queen mother Catherine de Médicis; her daughter-in-law Mary, Queen of Scots; and of course Elizabeth herself. Having women in positions of power made many people nervous. Scottish preacher John Knox, for example, wrote an angry pamphlet about the "monstrous regiment [rule] of women" during the reign of Elizabeth's half sister, Mary. Anxieties about women's roles and religious changes created a climate in which an odd or troublesome woman might easily be thought of as a witch.

Many people of all ranks and education levels in England believed that witches existed and that they used their powers to commit such evil deeds as raising storms, destroying crops, causing

The Church

illnesses, harming livestock, and drying up wells. Women accused of practicing witchcraft were usually older, poor, and lonely—often widows. Behaviors that commonly drew suspicion to them included begging, quarreling, swearing, and mumbling and grumbling (which may have sounded like they were muttering curses). There was at least one writer, though, who became skeptical about sorcerous goings-on. His name was Reginald Scot, and in his 1584 book *The Discoverie of Witchcraft* he wrote, "The fables of witchcraft have taken so fast hold and deep root in the heart of man that few or none can nowadays with patience endure the hand and correction of God." That is, people were blaming their misfortunes on witches instead of accepting that hardships were God's tests or punishments.

Catherine de Médicis was the mother of three successive kings of France and mother-in-law of a fourth. Her great influence over the French throne made her a controversial figure, and many blamed her for France's troubles during this period.

Scot did allow that now and then a woman might truly believe she was a witch, but he concluded that this was because she suffered from delusions due to a "melancholy humor"—in modern terms, depression or some other mental illness. Not everyone, however, accepted Scot's arguments. Exact figures are hard to come by, but we know that there were a number of witchcraft accusations and at least a few witch hunts in Elizabeth's England. Three of these hunts occurred in the southeastern county of Essex, resulting in the trials of one man and sixteen women. One of the women was tried twice, receiving a light sentence the first time and the death penalty the second. Seven others were hanged for witchcraft as a result of these hunts, but five were acquitted, and the fates of the others are unknown. England was a remarkably moderate nation during the witch-hunting craze of the time: in Germany, Switzerland, and France, thousands of accused witches were burned at the stake.

MAGIC, ASTROLOGY, AND SUPERSTITION

The Injunctions of 1559 stated, "no persons shall use charms, sorceries, enchantments, witchcraft, soothsaying [fortune-telling], or any suchlike devilish device, nor shall resort at any time to the same for counsel or help." The fact that this rule had to be made shows how common such practices were in 1559—and they continued to be popular throughout Elizabeth's reign. Many people believed in magic, which might be practiced by anyone from a country girl casting a love spell to a wealthy university graduate performing elaborate rituals in ancient languages to call upon powerful spiritual beings. Such a magician was the central character in Christopher Marlowe's famous play *Doctor Faustus*. Shakespeare's plays, too, often included magic or references to magic, reflecting the fascination Elizabethans felt for the subject.

Even though it could be used for "soothsaying," astrology enjoyed not only popularity but also respect. Queen Elizabeth had her own astrological adviser, Dr. John Dee, whom

she consulted on many occasions. It was he who determined the best date for Elizabeth's coronation, when the positions of the planets would be most favorable for the official beginning of a long and successful reign. Dee also had a reputation as a wizard. His expertise was sought whenever Elizabeth's councillors thought the queen was being threatened by magical means—for example, when they found a portrait of her with a pin stuck through it. Dee, along with Sir Walter Raleigh and Christopher Marlowe, was part of a group of learned men who regularly gathered in the 1580s to discuss philosophy, science, mathematics, alchemy, astrology, and theories of magic. In Elizabethan England, these topics were all closely related.

Above: John Dee was not only an astrologer but a noted mathematician, and was learned in other areas as well.

Magic and medicine mixed freely, too, with many remedies including the use of charms as well as herbal drugs. And there were all kinds of beliefs about luck and fate. For example, some people claimed you could know how many years you would live by counting the wrinkles on your forehead. It was bad luck to stumble in the doorway when leaving on a journey, or to have a hare cross your path. There were lucky and unlucky days to cut your nails, and much of your future could be predicted according to the day of the week you had been born on. Dreams, too, contained messages about coming events. Thunder could herald bad fortune—so you might want to pay attention to the number of times a crow cawed in the morning, which could foretell the weather for the day. A piece of unicorn horn or mandrake root, or a piece of jewelry or paper with appropriate symbols on it, could protect you from many sorts of danger and bad luck. Even Queen Elizabeth once gave the Earl of Essex a magical ring to shield him from the perils of a long journey. It may have been a kind of "joke gift"—but maybe not.

Above: This fifteenth-century manuscript shows an astrologer using an early form of telescope to examine the heavens. Mathematician Leonard Digges, a member of John Dee's group of scholarly friends, probably invented the first reflecting telescope in the 1550s.

5

Through Life's Stages

The parson, vicar, or curate, and parishioners of every parish within this realm,

shall in their churches and chapels keep one book or register, wherein they shall

write the day and year of every wedding, christening, and burial made within

their parish . . . and also therein shall write every person's name that

shall be so wedded, christened, and buried.

⁓ THE INJUNCTIONS OF 1559

THE CATHOLIC CHURCH HAD SEVEN RITES CALLED sacraments, ceremonies that both demonstrated God's grace and bestowed it on those taking part in the sacrament: Holy Communion, baptism, confirmation, penance (confession), marriage, extreme unction (anointing a dying person), and holy orders (for men joining the priesthood). The Church of England decreed that there were only two sacraments, Holy Communion and baptism, because only those had been instituted by Jesus. Nevertheless, the important stages in people's lives continued to be marked by special church services, as set down in the Book of Common Prayer.

Opposite: This famous painting by nineteenth-century artist John Constable shows Salisbury Cathedral. In its peaceful setting in southern England, it would have looked much the same in Elizabeth's time.

ON BEING BORN

Childbirth was full of religious meaning for families. The church taught that babies were the "fruit of marriage" and a blessing from God. Moreover, in giving birth, a woman both experienced the punishment for Eve's disobedience and received greater hope of salvation because she was bringing a new Christian into the world. Yet the baby entered life, like all human beings, in a state of sin and in need of God's grace. Access to this grace came through baptism (sometimes called christening), a ceremony that also made the newborn a member of the Christian community.

The beginning of the public baptism service made this clear: "Dearly beloved, forasmuch as all men be conceived and born in sin, . . . I beseech you to call upon God the father, through our lord Jesus Christ, that . . . he will grant to these children . . . that they may be baptized with water and the Holy Ghost, and

received into Christ's holy church." The child to be baptized was brought up to the font or basin at the front of the church by the godparents—traditionally two women and one man for a girl, and two men and one woman for a boy. The Book of Common Prayer instructed:

Family and friends gather for a feast to celebrate the christening of a baby, proudly held by its father.

> Then the priest shall take the child in his hands, and ask the name; and naming the child, shall dip it in the water, . . . saying, "*N.* [the child's name] I baptize thee in the name of the Father, and of the Son, and of the Holy Ghost. Amen." . . . Then the priest shall make a cross upon the child's forehead, saying, "We receive this child into the congregation of Christ's flock, and do sign him with the sign of the cross, in token that hereafter he shall not be ashamed to confess the faith of Christ crucified."

Babies were commonly baptized two or three days after birth, ideally on a Sunday or other holy day. But if it looked as though a newborn was going to die and there was no time to get to church or to summon a minister, anyone could baptize it. Usually such an emergency baptism would be done by the midwife or one of the other women helping the mother during childbirth. This was the only time a woman was allowed to perform any kind of religious service. Many bishops and ministers were uneasy with the practice, but to parents it could be a great comfort. Although church authorities mainly agreed that a baby who died unbaptized would not go to hell, ordinary people tended to believe that only baptized children would go to heaven. This was a real concern, because about 2 percent of infants died the day they were born, and another 3 percent died before the week was up.

Women, too, often died during or soon after childbirth. If the mother lived, she spent the next month (ideally, anyway) resting at home—she did not even go out to attend her baby's baptism. At the end of the month she went to church for the ceremony popularly known as churching. Its formal name was the Thanksgiving of Women after Childbirth. Her midwife and women friends accompanied her, and often they had a special pew to sit in at the front of the church. At a fitting point in the regular service, the minister called the new mother forward to kneel before the congregation. After reading one of the Psalms, he led everyone in a prayer thanking God for delivering "this woman thy servant from the great pain and peril of childbirth" and asking for his continued blessing on her. Churching marked a mother's full return to the community and the routines of everyday life. Like a baby's baptism, it was an occasion for feasting and merrymaking once the church service was done.

GROWING UP IN THE FAITH

Parents were expected to teach their children the basics of the Christian faith, starting as young as possible. In addition, on each holy day every minister was supposed to "hear and instruct all the youth of the parish for half an hour at the least before evening prayer, in the Ten Commandments, the Articles of Belief, and in the Lord's Prayer, and diligently examine them." For those children who went on to school, religious instruction was part of their education, as the Injunctions of 1559 urged: "All teachers of children shall stir and move them to the love and due reverence of God's true religion. . . . They shall accustom their scholars reverently to learn such sentences of Scriptures as shall be most expedient to induce them to all godliness."

This boy has probably just started wearing breeches (pants) instead of the long gowns of early childhood. At six or seven, he's now old enough to begin his formal education, which will include religious instruction.

In literate households, families often read the Bible together. The most commonly owned book in Elizabethan England was the Bible, and next was *Acts and Monuments* by John Foxe, popularly known as the *Book of Martyrs*. It told the stories of Protestants who had died for their faith, and it was favorite reading material for both children and adults. There was also an increasing number of what we might call inspirational advice books for parents. For instance, the following selection from John Lyster's *A Rule How to Bring Up Children* provides an example of how a father might discuss the scriptures with his son.

FATHER. The duty of parents would I learn, for many bring up their children wantonly. Tell me, therefore, plainly and truly: although thou be but a child in years, yet, I praise God, thou art almost a man in wisdom and understanding.

SON. The Lord said, I know that Abraham will command his children and his household after him, that they keep the way of the Lord, and do after right and conscience. *Genesis 13* . . . You shall, saith God, teach all my laws and ordinances unto your children. *Deuteronomy 4* . . .

FATHER. What saith the scripture of children to their parents?

SON. Thus saith St. Paul: children, obey your fathers and mothers in the Lord, for that is right. Honor thy father and mother that thou mayest prosper and live long on the earth. *Ephesians 6* . . . He that defieth his father shall come to shame, and he that forsaketh his mother is cursed of God. *Ecclesiastes 3*

MARRIAGE

Although marriage was not considered a sacrament, the Anglican Church taught that God himself had instituted it in paradise and that Jesus had blessed it by performing his first miracle at a wedding. Therefore people should marry "reverently, discreetly, advisedly, soberly, and in the fear of God." Marriage was for life—divorce was almost never allowed. A period of courtship was strongly encouraged so that a couple had a chance to get to know each other well enough to be reasonably sure they could get along till death parted them.

After a man and woman became formally engaged, their intention to marry had to be announced in church three Sundays in a row. This was called asking (or reading or publishing) the banns. Each time, as one Elizabethan author explained it, the priest asked the congregation "whether any man can allege a reason wherefore they that are about to be married may not lawfully come together." Possible reasons included: the couple were too closely related to each other, they were too young, they did not have the consent of their parents (necessary if they were under twenty-one), one of them was already married, or one of them was already engaged to someone else.

If a couple could not wait for the banns, for one reason or another, they could apply for a special marriage license. This

license was also necessary for anyone who wanted to marry at home or in a church other than their parish church, or to have their wedding during a time of year when marriages were not supposed to be performed. (These "forbidden seasons" were mainly the forty days before and eight days after Easter, and the month before and twelve days after Christmas.) To obtain a license, the couple had to pay a fee and swear to the bishop's representative that there was no lawful reason for them not to marry.

In the Book of Common Prayer's wedding service, couples promised faithfulness "for better, for worse . . . till death us depart."

With the banns or license taken care of, the couple could finally wed. After making a short statement about the basis of Christian marriage, the minister asked one last time if there was any reason why the couple could not lawfully marry. If no one spoke, the minister then asked the man, "Wilt thou have this woman to thy wedded wife . . . ? Wilt thou love her, comfort her, honor, and keep her, in sickness, and in health? And forsaking all other, keep thee only to her, so long as you both shall live?" The man answered, "I will," and the minister asked the woman the same question—with the addition of "Wilt thou obey him and serve him?"

The exchange of vows followed, each promising the other "to have and to hold from this day forward, for better, for worse, for richer, for poorer, in sickness, and in health, to love and to cherish, till death us depart." Again, the woman also promised "to obey." Then the man gave her the wedding ring. The minister said a short prayer, joined their right hands together, and declared, "Those whom God hath joined together, let no man put asunder," and pronounced them "man and wife."

The wedding service lasted no more than twenty minutes, unless there was Holy Communion or a sermon at its end. The celebration that followed, however, could go on for days, with processions, flowers, feasting, music, dancing, and gift giving all combining to help the newlyweds make a joyous start on their life together. There was often a lot of drinking and joking around, too, which both Puritans and church authorities disapproved of. An example was a man brought before the bishop's court for wearing women's clothing—he explained that he had been to a wedding and "in a merriment he did disguise himself in his wife's apparel to make some mirth to the company."

DEATH

Like baptism and marriage, death was a community event. When a person was seriously ill, people gathered around to give assistance and comfort. Often the minister was summoned to pray with the sick person, family, and neighbors: "Hear us, almighty and most merciful God . . . extend thy accustomed goodness to this thy servant which is grieved with sickness. . . . So visit and restore unto this sick person his former health (if it be thy will) or else give him grace . . . that after this painful life ended, he may dwell with thee in life everlasting." If the sick person desired it, the minister gave Holy Communion to everyone present.

As death neared, church bells rang to alert the parish that one of their neighbors was passing. Some people would pause in their work to pray for the sick person and perhaps to briefly contemplate the mysteries of death and life after death. Others would hurry to the bedside. Due to unhealthy conditions and lack of medical knowledge, the death rate was much higher in Elizabethan England than in developed nations today, so people confronted death frequently. They had a great interest in seeing how people died, because a "good death" was an inspiration to others, giving them courage to face the thought of their own life's eventual end.

After death, the body had to be washed and wrapped in a shroud or winding sheet. This was nearly always done by women—family members, servants, neighbors, or the local midwife. Sometimes the body was buried on the same day, almost always within two or three days. Between death and burial, there was often a night or two of "watching" the corpse. People sat up with the body, keeping each other company in their grief and praying. They were cautioned to pray *with* the dead, not *for* them. The Church of England taught that the souls of the dead went straight to heaven or hell, so that praying for them was both superstitious and useless. (In contrast, Catholics believed that after death souls went to purgatory, a place of suffering and cleansing before going to heaven, and that prayers by the living could lessen a soul's time there.) In some areas, espe-

THE QUEEN'S DEATH

When Queen Elizabeth lay dying in March 1603, she was surrounded by ladies-in-waiting, councillors, courtiers, and chaplains, with her favorite musicians playing soft music in the background. Archbishop John Whitgift was almost constantly at her side. Her cousin Robert Carey described the scene as the end drew near, when she had lost the ability to speak, but not to hear and understand:

Her Majesty lay upon her back, with one hand in the bed and the other without. The Archbishop kneeled down beside her and examined her first of her faith; and she so punctually answered all his questions, by lifting up her eyes and holding up her hand, as it was a comfort to all the beholders. Then the good man told her plainly what she was and what she was come to: though she had been long a great Queen here upon Earth, yet shortly she was to yield an account of her stewardship to the King of Kings. After this, he began to pray . . . with earnest cries to God for her soul's health, which he uttered with that fervency of spirit, as the Queen, to all our sight, much rejoiced thereat, and gave testimony to us all of her Christian and comfortable end.

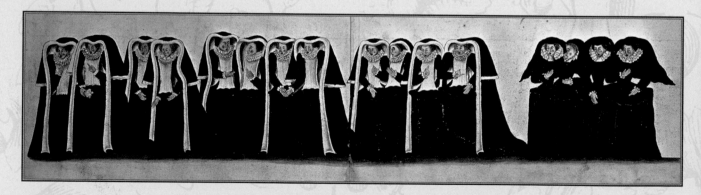

Elizabeth's ladies-in-waiting mourn the death of their beloved queen as they walk in her funeral procession.

cially among the common people, the watching turned into a festive occasion, with drinking, music, and games. This happened most often when the deceased had lived a long, full life and died peacefully. In the case of a tragic death, however, such as that of a child, the watching was always a solemn and grief-filled occasion.

The burial service was brief and simple. The minister greeted the funeral procession at the gate of the churchyard and read or sang a series of Bible verses about the Resurrection and the briefness of life on earth. He prayed as the body was laid in the grave, and then, as the mourners threw handfuls of dirt onto it, he said, "Forasmuch as it hath pleased almighty God of his great mercy to take unto himself the soul of our dear brother, here departed, we therefore commit his body to the ground, earth to earth, ashes to ashes, dust to dust, in sure and certain hope of resurrection to eternal life."

After more Bible readings and perhaps a sermon, the mourners went back to the home of the dead person for a funeral dinner. If the deceased had been well off, his will usually provided for giving food (and sometimes money) to the parish poor on this occasion, as in this example from 1561: "I ordain at my burial a solemn drinking to be made . . . , i.e. three fat sheep, three barrels of beer, and six dozen [loaves] of bread, to be provided for my poor and rich neighbours that will come to it."

6

Holy Days

All the queen's faithful and loving subjects shall from henceforth celebrate
and keep their holy day according to God's will and pleasure.
⁓ THE INJUNCTIONS OF 1559

"IS THIS A HOLIDAY?" ASKS A CHARACTER AT THE BEGIN-
ning of Shakespeare's play *Julius Caesar*. In Elizabethan England,
though, it was easy to tell—at least between 1571 and 1591. During
those twenty years, the law required every male above the age of six
and below the rank of gentleman to wear a knitted wool cap on
every holy day, including Sundays. This measure was disliked by the
men and boys who had to wear the caps, but it did help the English
wool trade. Similarly, Elizabeth's government boosted the nation's
fishing industry by mandating that people eat fish instead of meat
during Lent (the forty days before Easter)—and on all Wednesdays,
Fridays, and Saturdays as well. Church and state were as closely
joined on holy days as they were on every other day of the year.

Opposite: Crowned with
a wreath of holly, an
Elizabethan actor is ready
to play his part in a
Christmas celebration.

59

SOUL CAKES

On All Saints' Day many English housewives baked buns called soul cakes, which they gave out to visitors and the poor. Gradually a custom developed of children going door to door begging for soul cakes—the beginning of trick-or-treating. This recipe from 1604 is one that could have been used for these little cakes:

> Take flower [flour] & sugar & nutmeg & cloves, & mace, & sweet butter, & sack [sherry], & a little ale barme [used instead of yeast], beat your spice, & put in your butter, & your sack, cold, then work it well all together, & make it in little cakes, & so bake them, if you will you may put in some saffron into them or fruit.

An easy way to make your own soul cakes is to start with a mix, such as Pillsbury Hot Roll Mix. Put the dry ingredients into a bowl and add 1/4 cup sugar, 1/4 cup dried currants or raisins, and 1/4 teaspoon each of nutmeg, cloves, and mace. Then just follow the package instructions for mixing, shaping, and baking the rolls. Enjoy!

Above: The preparation of special foods made the kitchen an extra busy place at holiday time.

THE SABBATH

Sunday was the Sabbath, the weekly day of rest. English law followed biblical law in declaring that it should be kept holy (at least partly). Everyone was expected to be in church for the morning service, to praise God and to pray for his blessings and forgiveness:

> Almighty and most merciful father, we have erred and strayed from thy ways, like lost sheep we have followed too much the devices and desires of our own hearts. . . . We have left undone those things which we ought to have done, and we have done those things which we ought not to have done. . . . O Lord, have mercy upon us miserable offenders.

In every Sunday service there were readings from the Old Testament and New Testament, and the minister would either preach a sermon or read one from the Book of Homilies. Once a month Holy Communion was held; everyone was required to participate on Easter and at least two other times a year.

Communion, also called the Lord's Supper, was the church's most important rite. The Articles of Faith explained, "The Supper of the Lord is not only a sign of the love that Christians ought to have among themselves one to another; but rather it is a Sacrament of our Redemption by Christ's death: insomuch that . . . the Bread which we break is a partaking of the Body of Christ; and likewise the Cup of Blessing is a partaking of the Blood of Christ." Holy Communion was modeled on the Last Supper, Jesus's final meal with his disciples. He had given them bread and wine, declaring that these were his body and blood, and bid them eat and drink in memory of him. As the priest gave bread and wine to his congregation, he said, "Take and eat this in remembrance that Christ died for thee.

... Drink this in remembrance that Christ's blood was shed for thee, and be thankful." As these words indicate, Protestant communion was a symbolic act, whereas in Catholic teaching the bread and wine were mystically transformed into the actual body and blood of Jesus. This difference in interpretation of the sacrament was one of the most fundamental divisions between the churches.

In the Anglican Church people knelt together at the communion table during the Lord's Supper. But during the rest of the service, women and men usually sat in separate sections, and pews were assigned by social class—the higher in rank you were, the closer to the front your seat was. Apparently, this practice sometimes led people to forget their Christian love for each other and fight over where they deserved to sit. Ministers had other problems with their congregations, too. The "Homily on Repairing and Keeping Clean the Church" tried to deal with some of these issues, and concludes this way:

> Do ye your parts, good people, to keep your churches comely [attractive] and clean, suffer them not to be defiled with rain and weather, with dung of doves and owls. . . . It is the house of prayer, not the house of talking, of walking, of brawling, of minstrelsy, of hawks, of dogs. . . . But have God in your heart, be obedient to his blessed will, bind yourselves every man and woman, to your power, toward the reparations and clean keeping of the church . . . that ye may be the better encouraged to resort to your parish church, there to learn your duty towards God and your neighbor.

After the service, people were not supposed to do any work, although exceptions were made—for farmers during the harvest season, for example. Most people spent their Sunday afternoons in

games, dancing, and other forms of recreation. In 1585, however, Puritans in Parliament proposed a bill that would ban Sunday entertainments and sports. Queen Elizabeth refused to let it go forward—she felt that once her subjects had fulfilled their obligation to attend church, they should be able to enjoy the remainder of their day of rest as they saw fit. But Puritans still believed that everyone should spend the entire Sabbath in quiet and holy pastimes, and many people did choose to. For example, here is an entry from Lady Margaret Hoby's diary, in which she describes a routine Sunday:

Card playing was a popular form of indoor recreation. Here two ladies and two gentlemen enjoy a card party in a private room at an inn.

> After I was ready, I went to private prayers, then to breakfast; then I walked till church-time with Mr. Hoby, and after to

dinner. After which I walked and had speech of no serious matters till 2 o'clock. Then I writ notes in my bible till 3. And after 4 I came again from the church, walked and meditated a little and again writ some other notes in my Bible of that I had learned till 5, at which time I returned to examination and prayer. And after I had read some of the Bond of the Sabbath, I walked abroad. And so to supper, after to prayers and lastly to bed.

HOLIDAYS

When England was Catholic, there were nearly a hundred holy days in addition to Sundays—all days when no work was to be done and everyone was expected to attend church. The Church of England reduced the number to twenty-seven, eliminating nearly all saints' days. The holidays that were left commemorated events in the lives of Jesus and his mother, Mary; Jesus's twelve disciples; the authors of the Gospels (the first four books of the New Testament); the first Christian martyr (Saint Stephen); and the archangel Michael. All the other saints were remembered together on All Saints' Day, November 1.

From a religious viewpoint, the most important holiday was Easter Sunday. This was the celebration of Jesus's Resurrection, the event that gave Christians the promise of eternal life. People marked the day by taking Holy Communion, and there would probably be special hymns and sermons in church. Outside church, some people might observe the springtime tradition of decorating their houses with fresh greenery. They may also have given each other Easter eggs—this, too, was an old custom in England. Another tradition was observed by the queen on the Thursday before Easter, known as Maundy Thursday. This day was the commemoration of Jesus's Last Supper, at which he washed the feet of his disciples. Every year in memory of this, the queen ceremoniously washed the feet of a number of poor women, then gave them gifts of bread, fish, cheese, wine, cloth, and money.

The other great holiday was Christmas, the celebration of Jesus's birth. Christmas Day itself was devoted mainly to church, and many people participated in Communion. After church there would be a family dinner, perhaps featuring a roast turkey—the New World bird had been introduced to Europe in the early 1500s and was a popular Christmas food in Elizabethan England. Then on December 26, Saint Stephen's Day, the Twelve Days of Christmas began a period of feasting, dancing, visiting, gift giving, pageants, and general merriment. This verse by poet George Wither captures the spirit of the season:

Court artist and lady-in-waiting Levina Teerlinc made this miniature painting of one of Queen Elizabeth's Maundy Thursday ceremonies around 1560. Elizabeth is on the lower left, wearing a white apron and a skirt with a long blue train that is carried by one of her ladies. The poor women whose feet she will wash are seated along the left side of the scene.

> So now is come our joyful'st feast,
> Let every man be jolly.
> Each room with ivy leaves is drest,
> And every post with holly.
> > Though some churls at our mirth repine,
> > Round your foreheads garlands twine,
> > Drown sorrow in a cup of wine,
> And let us all be merry.

7

Conflict and Challenge

Forbear to judge, for we are sinners all.
— SHAKESPEARE, *2 HENRY VI*

T HE ORDERLY SWITCH FROM CATHOLICISM TO THE Church of England worked because of the common sense and moderation of Elizabeth and her advisers and because of their and the people's desire for a peaceful nation. Yet there were still problems. Puritans believed Elizabeth had not reformed the church enough. Catholics felt she had gone too far. Even those in the middle sometimes missed aspects of the old faith. For example, the author of the "Homily of the Place and Time of Prayer" reported overhearing a woman say to her friend, "Alas . . . what shall we now do at Church, since all the Saints are taken away, since all the goodly sights we were wont to have are gone, since we cannot hear the like piping, singing, chanting, and playing upon the organs that we could before." The changes took time—decades, in some parishes—to get used to.

Opposite: Puritan clergymen sometimes preached fiery sermons that inspired their congregations to destroy organs, statues, stained-glass windows, and other works of art in churches.

EXTREME PROTESTANTS

For the first ten years of Elizabeth's religious settlement, there were relatively few problems. The greatest difficulties were with Puritans who got carried away with removing statues, altars, and other decorations from the churches. They often ended up destroying a great deal of priceless artwork and other church property, including monuments to the dead. In many places, such as Shakespeare's hometown of Stratford-upon-Avon, they smashed stained-glass windows, even though the laws allowed these to remain.

Most people with Puritan ideas made their peace with the practices of the Church of England. Elizabeth's Puritan councillor Sir Francis Walsingham expressed a common attitude when he advised, "Thank God for what we presently enjoy, having God's word sincerely preached and the Sacraments truly administered. . . . The rest we lack we are to beg by prayer and attend [wait] with patience." Some Puritan ministers and parishioners, though, defied the rules in various ways—for example, by refusing to make the sign of the cross over babies at baptism or by omitting the wedding ring from the marriage ceremony. If minister and parishioner shared the same views and were discreet, they could get away with it. But where there was disagreement between priests and their congregations, those who refused to follow the Book of Common Prayer could be reported to the bishop's court for discipline. This was a sore point, too, for many Puritans wanted to do away with bishops completely and let each congregation govern itself.

Although his personal religious beliefs were Puritan, Sir Francis Walsingham was completely loyal to Elizabeth and shared her commitment to keeping England free of religious strife.

Puritans caused other difficulties when they tried to force their strict interpretation of Christianity on government and society. One Puritan minister campaigned to have adultery, heresy, and blasphemy punished by death, as commanded in the Old Testament. Another wrote a letter to the queen to scold her for swearing, and still another preached her a sermon about "the vanity of decking the body too finely." There were numerous Puritan attempts to outlaw such things as May Day games and dances, excessive holiday feasting, fancy wedding and funeral processions, and, above all, plays and pageants.

Queen Elizabeth, however, loved gathering flowers and dancing on May Day, watching plays, and taking part in all kinds of feasting and festivities. She knew how much pleasure these things could give, and how much the traditional customs mattered to the average English person. In 1575, for instance, a group of men from the city of Coventry complained to her that they were no longer allowed to present their annual historical pageant. "They knew no cause why . . . unless it were by the zeal of certain of their preachers, men very commendable for behavior and learning, and sweet in their sermons, but somewhat too sour in preaching away their pastime." Elizabeth saw to it that the pageant was reinstated. Similarly, when there was trouble over maypole dancing in the 1580s, her Privy Council issued the statement, "We see no cause that these pastimes of recreation, being not used at unlawful times . . . [nor] in disordered and riotous sort, shall be forbidden to the people."

WARRING FAITHS

After Elizabeth's death, the Puritans would become more powerful, even ruling the country during the mid-1600s. During Elizabeth's reign, the greater problem was with Catholics, both within and outside her realm. At first, she allowed English Catholics a limited freedom of religion: so long as they publicly attended and supported the Church of England, they were free to worship as they chose privately. At the time, this was much more tolerance than other Protestant nations gave to Catholics, and more than Catholic nations gave to Protestants. Elizabeth was interested in maintaining peace and order, not in forcing people to match their personal beliefs with hers.

But then in 1570, the pope issued a decree that declared Elizabeth a heretic—a breaker of God's laws and destroyer of the church. Because of this, the pope said, her Catholic subjects did not owe her their loyalty. In fact, they had an obligation to disobey her and her laws: "She has forfeited her pretended title to the aforesaid kingdom, and is deprived of all dominion, dignity, and privilege. We declare that nobles, subjects, and peoples are free from any oath to her, and we interdict [forbid] obedience to her. . . ." Perhaps the pope was trying to pressure Elizabeth into rejoining the Catholic Church. Instead, he set up a situation in which every English Catholic was a potential enemy of queen and country. English Catholics themselves were forced into the uncomfortable position of being traitors either to their country or their church—although most were able to make compromises that at least satisfied their own consciences.

Fear and suspicion of Catholics grew steadily from this point on. In 1571 Parliament made it treason to bring copies of the pope's decrees into England or to call the queen a heretic. The next year, the English were shaken by news of the Saint Bartholomew's Day

Pope Pius V, who labeled Elizabeth a heretic and encouraged English Catholics to rebel against her

Massacre, in which nearly ten thousand Protestants were killed by Catholic mobs in France. The pope gave public thanks for the French king's role in destroying "the enemies of Christ." Francis Walsingham, England's ambassador to France at the time, wrote home, "Can we think that the fire kindled here in France will extend itself no further?"

Tensions built over the next decade. Catholic missionaries began to arrive in England and were secretly welcomed into many homes and communities. Evidence mounted that there were both English and foreign Catholics plotting to overthrow Elizabeth and put her Catholic cousin Mary, Queen of Scots, on the throne instead. In 1580 the pope declared that it would not be a sin to kill Elizabeth; several attempts on her life followed almost immediately. In 1581 Parliament made it high treason to convert to Catholicism or to try to convert any English person to Catholicism. The fine for not attending Anglican services was raised to twenty pounds—more than the average university graduate earned in a year. Soon it became treason simply to be a Catholic priest, and giving help or shelter to a Catholic priest was punishable by death.

The Saint Bartholomew's Day Massacre (August 24, 1572) was one of the most tragic events of Elizabeth's time. She and her advisers were determined to keep anything similar from happening in England.

A shepherd's thoughts turn to praising God
as he watches over his flock.

COMFORT IN TROUBLED TIMES

The Injunctions of 1559 instructed ministers to "have always in readiness such comfortable [comforting] places and sentences of Scripture, as do set forth the mercy, benefits, and goodness of Almighty God . . . that they may at all times when necessity shall require, promptly comfort their flock with the lively [living] word of God." No doubt one of the scriptures the Injunctions had in mind was Psalm 23, "The Lord Is My Shepherd." Here is a verse translation made by Sir Philip Sidney.

1. The Lord, the Lord my shepherd is,
   And so can never I
     Taste misery.
   He rests me in green pasture His;
     By waters still and sweet
       He guides my feet.

2. He me revives, leads me the way
   Which righteousness doth take,
     For His name's sake.
   Yea, though I should through valleys stray
     Of death's dark shade, I will
       No whit fear ill.

3. For Thou, dear Lord, Thou me besett'st;
     Thy rod and Thy staff be
       To comfort me:
   Before me thou a table sett'st,
     Even when foes' envious eye
       Doth it espy.

4. Thou oil'st my head, Thou fill'st my cup;
     Nay, more, Thou endless good
       Shalt give me food:
   To Thee, I say, ascended up,
     Where Thou, the Lord of all,
       Dost hold thy hall.

In 1588, King Philip II of Spain, with the pope's blessing and financial support, attempted to invade England and reclaim it for the Catholic Church. The English navy defeated his fleet, the Spanish Armada. During the crisis of wartime, English Catholics and Protestants fought side by side to preserve their country's freedom. Indeed, most English Catholics were completely loyal to Elizabeth throughout her reign. The actions of a few, unfortunately, put suspicion on all—even after the defeat of the Armada. Catholicism and the people who practiced it were felt to be such a threat that it would be more than two hundred years before Catholics would enjoy full freedom of religion in England.

Elizabeth had wanted to keep her country united by steering a middle course between Catholicism and extreme Protestantism. In large measure, she was successful. This success, however, sometimes came at a high price—her reign saw nearly two hundred Catholics, mostly priests, executed for treason. In England as elsewhere, church and state were too closely linked during this period for religious tolerance to prevail.

Yet from the troubles of Elizabeth's time came the seeds of a new way of thinking about the relationships between religion, government, and society. More people came to value freedom of worship and to believe that religion was a matter of individual conscience rather than government control. People also began to see that a government controlled by religion would not be able to properly serve all the people of the nation, with their diversity of beliefs and opinions. Within fifty years of the great queen's death, the seeds of these ideas would start bearing fruit in England's colonies in North America, where separation of church and state would eventually become one of the cornerstones of freedom.

GLOSSARY

Catholic refers to the branch of Christianity under the authority of the pope

chaplain a clergyman who served in the private chapel of a ruler, noble, or bishop

congregation the group of people who attend a particular church

ecclesiastical (from *ecclesia*, Latin for "church") having to do with the church

humanism an approach to learning that emphasized study of the subjects known as the humanities: grammar (Latin and Greek in particular), rhetoric (the art of persuasive speaking and writing), literature, philosophy, and history

Low Countries today's Netherlands and Belgium. During Elizabeth's time they were ruled by Spain.

manuscript a handwritten book

martyr someone who is killed because of their religion

militia a locally based armed force made up regular citizens (as opposed to professional soldiers). In Elizabethan England, all able-bodied males aged sixteen to sixty might be required to serve in the militias in a national emergency.

missionaries people who travel to teach their religion to the people of another place

Parliament the legislative branch of the English government, made up of the House of Commons and the House of Lords. In Elizabeth's time, it only met when the monarch summoned it, and its main function was to approve taxes and major changes in policy.

Privy Council the queen's closest advisers, who ran government departments and saw that her decisions were put into effect

Protestant refers to Christians who reject the authority of the pope and many practices and beliefs of the Catholic Church

Psalms a book of the Bible containing songlike poems of prayer and praise

Puritan a Protestant who wanted to rid church and society of everything non-biblical. Elizabethans sometimes referred to Puritans as "precisionists." Most Puritans remained within the Church of England, but a small proportion wanted their own, separate churches.

Reformation the movement begun in 1517 by Martin Luther to reform the Catholic Church. Eventually the Reformation resulted in the founding of many different Christian groups, such as Lutherans, Anglicans (Episcopalians), Calvinists (Presbyterians), and Baptists.

The Church

tithe a tax collected by the church. It was supposed to be one-tenth of a household's income.

FOR FURTHER READING

Adams, Simon. *Elizabeth I: The Outcast Who Became England's Queen.* Washington, DC: National Geographic, 2005.

Ashby, Ruth. *Elizabethan England.* New York: Benchmark Books, 1999.

Greenblatt, Miriam. *Elizabeth I and Tudor England.* New York: Benchmark Books, 2002.

Hinds, Kathryn. *Life in the Renaissance: The Church.* New York: Benchmark Books, 2004.

Lace, William W. *Defeat of the Spanish Armada.* San Diego: Lucent Books, 1997.

Lace, William W. *Elizabethan England.* San Diego: Lucent Books, 2005.

ONLINE INFORMATION

BBC. *British History: Tudors.*
   http://www.bbc.co.uk/history/british/tudors

Monson, Shelly. *Elizabethan Holiday Customs.*
   http://guildofstgeorge.com/holiday.htm

Renaissance: The Elizabethan World.
   http://elizabethan.org

Thomas, Heather. *The Elizabethan Church.*
   http://www.elizabethi.org/us/elizabethanchurch/

SELECTED BIBLIOGRAPHY

The 1559 Book of Common Prayer. Edited by Charles Wohlers.
   http://justus.anglican.org/resources/bcp/1559/BCP_1559.htm

The Anglican Library, ed. *The Homilies.* HTML edition, 1999.
   http://www.anglicanlibrary.org/homilies

Budiansky, Stephen. *Her Majesty's Spymaster: Elizabeth I, Sir Francis Walsingham, and the Birth of Modern Espionage.* New York: Viking, 2005.

Cressy, David. *Birth, Marriage and Death: Ritual, Religion, and the Life-Cycle in Tudor and Stuart England.* Oxford: Oxford University Press, 1997.

Dunn, Jane. *Elizabeth and Mary: Cousins, Rivals, Queens.* New York: Knopf, 2004.

Durant, Will, and Ariel Durant. *The Age of Reason Begins.* New York: Simon and Schuster, 1961.

Greenblatt, Stephen. *Will in the World: How Shakespeare Became Shakespeare.* New York: W. W. Norton, 2004.

The Injunctions of 1559. In Henry Gee and W. H. Hardy, eds., *Documents Illustrative of English Church History.* New York, 1896. Placed online by Hanover

Historical Texts Project, 1998.
http://history.hanover.edu/texts/ENGref/er78.html

Orlin, Lena Cowen. *Elizabethan Households: An Anthology.* Washington, DC: The Folger Shakespeare Library, 1995.

Picard, Liza. *Elizabeth's London: Everyday Life in Elizabethan London.* New York: St. Martin's Press, 2003.

Pritchard, R. E., ed. *Shakespeare's England: Life in Elizabethan and Jacobean Times.* Stroud, Gloucestershire: Sutton Publishing, 1999.

Rowse, A. L. *The England of Elizabeth: The Structure of Society.* Madison: University of Wisconsin Press, 1978.

Weir, Alison. *The Life of Elizabeth I.* New York: Ballantine Books, 1998.

SOURCES FOR QUOTATIONS

This series of books tries to bring the people of Elizabethan England to life by quoting their own words whenever possible. All Shakespeare quotations are from William Shakespeare, *Complete Works, Compact Edition*, edited by Stanley Wells et al. (Oxford: Clarendon Press, 1988).

Chapter 1

p. 9 "O Lord our heavenly": "Prayer for the Queenes Majesty" in *The 1559 Book of Common Prayer* (spelling modernized).

p. 10 "That state could never": Durant, *The Age of Reason Begins,* p. 18.

p. 12 "an act restoring": "Elizabeth I's Act of Supremacy," available online at http://www.britainexpress.com/History/tudor/supremacy-text.htm

p. 13 "I . . . do utterly testify": ibid.

p. 13 "shall in any Enterludes": "An Act for the Uniformity of Common Prayer, and Service in the Church, and Administration of the Sacraments, 1559," available online at http://www.fordham.edu/halsall/mod/1559actofuniformity.html

p. 14 "There is only one": Weir, *The Life of Elizabeth I,* p. 54.

p. 15 "Of necessity there must": *The 1559 Book of Common Prayer* (spelling and punctuation modernized).

p. 17 "Let your Highness assure": Rowse, *The England of Elizabeth,* p. 397.

p. 17 "depopulations and devastations": ibid., p. 303.

Chapter 2

p. 19 "Almighty God will have": Anglican Library, *The Homilies* (spelling modernized).

p. 20 "The heavens themselves": Shakespeare, *Troilus and Cressida,* act 1, scene 3.

p. 22 "a sheet": Picard, *Elizabeth's London,* p. 259.

p. 24 "Churches were made": "Of the Place and Time of Prayer," Anglican
     Library, *The Homilies* (spelling modernized).

p. 24 "Let us honor and worship": "Homily against Peril of Idolatry," Anglican
     Library, *The Homilies* (spelling and punctuation modernized).

p. 25 "the laymen's books" and "no true image": ibid.

p. 26 "Whereas there was wont": Pritchard, *Shakespeare's England,* p. 108.

p. 27 "In all my travels": Weir, *The Life of Elizabeth I,* p. 252.

Chapter 3

p. 29 "They ought to excel": *The Injunctions of 1559.*

p. 32 "By this means": Rowse, *The England of Elizabeth,* p. 428.

p. 32 "He is a common": ibid., p. 423.

p. 34 "Do not, as some": Shakespeare, *Hamlet,* act 1, scene 3.

p. 34 "Ecclesiastical persons": *The Injunctions of 1559.*

p. 34 "preaching every Sabbath": Rowse, *The England of Elizabeth,* p. 432.

p. 35 "Because through lack" and "leisurely, plainly": *The Injunctions of 1559.*

Chapter 4

p. 37 "From woman sprang": Jane Anger, *Her Protection for Women,* available
     online at http://www.pinn.net/~sunshine/book-sum/anger1.html

p. 38 "the church of God": Anglican Library, *The Homilies* (spelling and punctu-
     ation modernized).

p. 38 "Thus doth Saint Peter": ibid.

p. 39 "He thereby setteth" and "that is the greatest": ibid.

p. 39 "if thou canst suffer": ibid.

p. 39 "You could seldom": Orlin, *Elizabethan Households,* pp. 36-37.

p. 40 "All married men": ibid., p. 41.

p. 41 "Thou has done me": Dunn, *Elizabeth and Mary,* p. 109.

p. 43 "The fables of witchcraft": Picard, *Elizabeth's London,* p. 278.

p. 44 "no persons shall use": *The Injunctions of 1559.*

Chapter 5

p. 47 "The parson, vicar": *The Injunctions of 1559.*

p. 48 "fruit of marriage": Cressy, *Birth, Marriage and Death,* p. 17.

p. 48 "Dearly beloved, forasmuch": *The 1559 Book of Common Prayer* (spelling
     and punctuation modernized).

p. 49 "Then the priest": ibid.

p. 50 "this woman thy servant": ibid.

p. 51 "hear and instruct" and "All teachers": *The Injunctions of 1559.*

p. 52 "FATHER. The duty": Orlin, *Elizabethan Households,* pp. 63–64.

p. 52 "reverently, discreetly": *The 1559 Book of Common Prayer* (spelling and
     punctuation modernized).

p. 53 "whether any man": Cressy, *Birth, Marriage and Death,* p. 305.

p. 53 "Wilt thou," etc.: *The 1559 Book of Common Prayer* (spelling modernized).

p. 54 "in a merriment": Cressy, *Birth, Marriage and Death,* p. 354.

p. 55 "Hear us, almighty": *The 1559 Book of Common Prayer* (spelling and punctuation modernized).

p. 56 "Her Majesty lay": Weir, *The Life of Elizabeth I,* p. 484.

p. 57 "Forasmuch as it hath pleased": *The 1559 Book of Common Prayer* (spelling and punctuation modernized).

p. 57 "I ordain": Cressy, *Birth, Marriage and Death,* p. 445.

Chapter 6

p. 59 "All the queen's faithful": *The Injunctions of 1559.*

p. 59 "Is this": Shakespeare, *Julius Caesar,* act 1, scene 1.

p. 60 "Take flower & sugar": from *Elinor Fettiplace's Receipt Book,* quoted at http://guildofstgeorge.com/recipes.htm#Soul

p. 61 "Almighty and most merciful": *The 1559 Book of Common Prayer* (spelling modernized).

p. 61 "The Supper of the Lord": *The Thirty-Nine Articles,* available online at http://www.fordham.edu/halsall/mod/1571-39articles.html

p. 61 "Take and eat": *The 1559 Book of Common Prayer* (spelling modernized).

p. 62 "Do ye your parts": Anglican Library, *The Homilies* (spelling and punctuation modernized).

p. 63 "After I was ready": Rowse, *The England of Elizabeth,* p. 482.

p. 65 "So now is come": "A Christmas Carol," available online at http://elizabethan.org/compendium/63.html

Chapter 7

p. 67 "Forbear to judge": Shakespeare, *2 Henry VI,* act 3, scene 3.

p. 67 "Alas . . . what shall": Anglican Library, *The Homilies* (spelling and punctuation modernized).

p. 68 "Thank God for what": Budiansky, *Her Majesty's Spymaster,* p. 39.

p. 69 "the vanity of decking": Weir, *The Life of Elizabeth I,* p. 56.

p. 69 "They knew no cause": Greenblatt, *Will in the World,* p. 44.

p. 69 "We see no cause": Rowse, *The England of Elizabeth,* p. 182.

p. 70 "She has forfeited": Budiansky, *Her Majesty's Spymaster,* p. 102.

p. 71 "the enemies": ibid., p. 17.

p. 71 "Can we think": ibid., p. 27.

p. 72 "have always in readiness": *The Injunctions of 1559.*

p. 72 "The Lord, the Lord": Sidney, *The Psalmes of David,* available online at http://uoregon.edu/%7Ebear/sidpsalms.html (spelling modernized).

INDEX

ABOUT THE AUTHOR

KATHRYN HINDS grew up near Rochester, NY. In college she studied music, writing, and religion, and went on to do graduate work in comparative literature and medieval studies. She has written more than twenty-five books for young people, including the books in the series LIFE IN ANCIENT EGYPT, LIFE IN THE ROMAN EMPIRE, LIFE IN THE RENAISSANCE, and LIFE IN THE MIDDLE AGES. Kathryn lives in the north Georgia mountains with her husband, their son, and an assortment of cats and dogs. When she is not reading or writing, she enjoys spending time with her family and friends, dancing, knitting, gardening, and taking walks in the woods. Visit her online at http://www.kathrynhinds.com

Fox Gradin, Celestial Studios Photography